To Malik

The Facts

By:

Stacy St. Hilaire

Contents

Fact(s) Definition

Dictionary Definition

Fact (noun): A thing that is indisputably the case

New York City Definition

Fact(s) (noun): Still something that is indisputably the case, but used more like an opinion or an affirmation

Example:

Person 1: Tourists dead be standing in the middle of the street taking pictures, and have the nerve to look at you funny when you walk by like you don't have somewhere to be.

Person 2: Facts B. Tourists dead be buggin.

A Letter to My Readers

Dear Readers,

I did this for you. Yes, you. I wrote this for my hardworking people who love to read, but do not have time to read a novel or invest in a plot. I also wrote this for the kids in the hood who are tired of reading the works of dead white men and want a piece of their culture or history reflected. I also wrote this for my kids living in neighborhoods with no diversity save the adopted Black or Asian kid. But mostly this is for anyone who is willing to read what I have to say and who believes in freedom of speech—and that transcends many divides.

I wish everyone could live in my world and see all the beauty and talent that I get to see. Growing up in New York City, there is music pouring through the streets, and people dancing outside, and beat boxing, and spitting bars (freestyle rapping). There's merengue, bachata, dancehall, reggae, hip hop, R&B, and more. There's so much self-expression all around for you to see. Whether rich or poor, New York City is an artistic hub. Events like "Shether" by Remy Ma or "Damn" by Kendrick Lamar being released are a big deal, just like when your talented homies make a movie or drop a song about the block, or do a mural. This is who we are: survivors, hustlers, artists, New Yorkers.

This is a special time we are living in. History happens every day. No one who has ever made history ever thought, "Years later they are going to be calling this (the golden age, the civil rights era, the renaissance, etc.)." We are living in an era of constant change. Many people view this flux as unstable and inherently a downward spiral, but behind every threat is an opportunity. When 2017 started I had no idea

7

what was in store. Many people welcomed President Trump; many people feared this America; many people abhorred it. We cannot deny the facts: Hate crimes have risen, as has fear, racism, and visible divisiveness; however, Americans have also started to rally more around causes they believe in. Alongside all the visible signs of supporting Trump are people with signs that say "coexist" and "hate has no home here." In short, in the beginning of Trump's era as president, we are seeing more and more Americans exercising their first amendment rights. Many people are taking freedom of expression too far and abusing it—hence the rise in hate crimes. Many people see this as a signal for change (whatever that means for them). Then, of course, you have the people who never do anything but complain. Say what you want and think what you want, this is a very special time that we are living in: a time where almost anything is

8

possible. So I have decided to join my fellow Americans in expressing myself with this collection of poems.

In a year where Prodigy has died, Kathy Griffin posed with a severed Trump head, and Miley Cyrus is an out and proud pansexual who quit drugs and has gone back to her country roots, I have decided to add my Americana to the mix. I come from a place where people are from all around the world: from Jamaica, from Mali, from Puerto Rico, from Bangladesh, or from Florida, from everywhere. People bring their pride to New York City streets. They bring their music and their culture; they bring their language and their food. In my limited travels I have met so many people from so many different walks of life, from my manager at my old campus job whose family came to America in 1644, to my friend Brooke, who is of Irish descent, whose family came to America in 1880, to my own family who made their appearance in more like 1980. Each individual person carries with them their own history, their own views of right and wrong, and their own dreams.

Here in America, we tend to see respecting individuality as other people respecting our own individuality. We do not practice respecting individuality as respecting that everyone is an individual and honoring that difference. Yet if we are truly being the America we say we are then we should be adapting Voltaire and preaching: I may not like the kind of individual you are, but I will defend to the death your right to exist as you are. If we are going to do this then we have to recognize how we define words like "fact" and "truth." For example, pie is delicious is an opinion, but is it true? If a person says "I like pie" then it is a fact that they like pie. It is then also true that they think pie is delicious. If another person says "I hate pie" and they think that pie is disgusting, well then it is a fact that they do not like pie. It is also true that they think pie is disgusting. However, pie being disgusting or delicious by itself are both opinions, and, therefore, can never be neither true nor false. Such is the nature of humanity. Everyone has their own personal truths that clash, sometimes viscerally, with what others hold to be true. We need to recognize that if we are serious about being a country built on upholding individuality, then we need to learn how to respect individuals. Perhaps to do that we should stop framing people's life truths as a "difference of opinion" and start framing them as a fact; because, it is a fact that they exist and that they exist both apart and beside us in this world, as well as differently. Once we wrap our heads around this fully then we can respect one another in our full humanity, and

11

work with each other. We are all different, but we all have something unique we bring to the table, and it is time we start recognizing and respecting that. Facts.

–Stacy

Alternative Facts

The facts have no alternative in my head
The alternative to facts mean that democracy is dead
If we are alternating facts with lies we cannot get
    ahead
We all must search for the truth as it will not be spoon
    fed

"Intelligence plus character: that is the true goal of

education."-**MLK**

Equity in Education

Denial of education is a civil rights violation
Poor or rich we deserve an education
We can't live in a country that claims to be free
While our minds aren't free to grow
The more you know the better your actions
The more knowledge the less B.S. factions
And more "I, Too, Sing America": truly America
Not their America or their version of America
That alienation America but the "I Have a Dream"
    America
That *Declaration of Sentiments and Resolutions*
    America
That "Gettysburg Address" and that "Hope" speech
    America
That we are visionary we are all America
We're tired of living in "Strange Fruit" America
Instead of education we live in let 'em hang America

Make America Great Again

Amurica
A place where the men are men
The women are women
And the niggers are niggers
Figures
Where'd that go?
We need to have that back
Let's go back to the past!
There lies all the answers to a positive future
That's always where innovation comes from
Who needs new?
In with the old
Bigotry is always in fashion
Just worn differently
Knock the dust off old ideas
See if it works differently this time
Give it the old college try
This is the American way
We stay the same
We "function" that way

White Niggas

They had different skin colors
But were in the same class
And to leave class one needs a pass
Permission granted

Beg to differ but they were different
Yet still the same
Two different skin colors
But they call each one the same name
Every time they horse around
And play their games

No exclusions, No sins
There was permission
They're known where they roam
So no one asks "Where's your pass?"
They know
So they get comfortable forgetting the past
It is not theirs but it is ours
So they live in forgetful bliss
Until a naive encounter

They look and see new niggas
New homies to have
But they aren't from the same block
So they don't know of their pass
Both see new people, each with their own past
But one greets the other with "my nigga" and opens
     up wounds from the past

They heard themselves use a familiar greeting
They can't understand the beef to be had with these
    new niggas
But they left school and forgot (the) class
"'My niggas?' Where's your pass, and did we write
    it?"
Are all passes universally recognized?

Black people do not agree on N word use
The NAACP buried it, they say it has no use
Meanwhile the younger gen never tires from its use
"We took the fire pin out of the grenade"
But it is still a grenade

In a white mouth it's still loaded
"Niggas" is still a gun
Your black friends gave it to you unloaded
But the "new niggas" weren't the ones
You didn't show your pass
You ignored the past
Now you aim your gun you think is empty
But the "new niggas" just see a gun

You're white.
Newsflash: Race in America is Not Dead
You saw black so you called them your niggas instead
But they heard a cracker cracking a whip in the past
Your white skin+that word still means hate
That time hasn't passed

All future friendship opportunities with these "new
    niggas" is dead
You wanted to be friends
But they heard racism instead

17

Designated White Person

I'm irresponsible colored
So I decided to black responsibly
I keep me a Designated White Person
Easily
My name is Stacy
From the inner city but they called me "Oreo"
White people love me so they gave me a pass
I speak white and they knew me from class
And white people love my personality
They don't apologize
And neither do I
So they kindly escort their black friend
When white people ask
"No she's not like them"
What are "they" like?
That's not their problem
But when their nigga is harassed they step up and
    defend

My America

My America is a land of equality
My America is a land of opportunity
My America is diverse
My America is one for all
My America is safe
My America is beautiful
My America has great education
My America is free for all
My America is a great place to live
My America is the best place to be who you are
My America is the leader of the world
My America is the standard other countries measure
    themselves by
My America is the best place in the world
But we don't live in my America
We live in their America
Because America isn't ours
It's theirs
It isn't fair
It isn't just
It isn't understanding
We can't all be who we are
Some of us can live
But the rest we don't let live
This is not the America we were promised
But it is the America we always had
It's not okay to be brown
It's not okay to be gay
It's not okay to poor
It's not okay to be asexual
It's not okay to be disabled
It's not okay to be Jewish
It's not okay to be Muslim

It's not okay to be a woman
It's not okay to be trans
It's not okay to be non-binary
What happened to equality?
Why do we argue over rights?
It's equality for everyone
In my America
Not real America
Guess America is not real America
We lie to ourselves
We lie to the world
We pretend to be evolved while remaining archaic
We the proud barbarians
The best at being contrary
The best at being revolutionary
We the game changers
Have failed to change the game
To beat the world
As of late
Because our practice is dusty
So we're eating the world's dust
We need to shake off the rust
We need to change the game before the game changes
    us
We need to run towards the America promised
Not the one of the past

Crooked smile, Straight Intentions

I got a crooked smile but straight intentions
I spit the straight facts they don't mention
I see past the front-cover to reality
I challenge assumptions to discover actuality
Like Maslow's hierarchy I'm tryna self-actualize
That's why when I talk all I do is try to factualize
All the lies that we have been led to believe
Straight smile crooked intentions make the whole
    world bleed
My daddy told me they were two tongued like a snake
Truth and lies make a stew in their mouth, but no
    mistakes
The lies are all in the brew and they come out with
    straight intention
Misleading the direction talking bout go "Weast" like
    Patrick's directions
Time to set the record straight without the click bait
    or the hate
It's time we take charge of the world, of love, of
    peace, and of fate

White Nation, One Nation

They try to deindividualize through lies
One lens
Telling us white is the best
No one can contest
Period

Black men shave your curls
Black women straighten or hide yours
No braids
That's too unprofessional
But wait
Twists and dreads are unprofessional
Too
Much expression of your self
Who you were born
Is less
You're a mess
See your head?
It's a nest
You animals
Savages
We are civilized
See how we keep it straight?
It's not the look we hate
It's what it symbolizes:
Difference

Difference is a threat in our minds
Yours too
It is a threat
To your values, sense of beauty, sense of excellence,
    sense of self
This cannot be allowed
No way in hell
Then everyone would think anything goes
Then order goes
Down the toilet
It's a swirl
Like curls
That's a no

Except media, art, and fashion are a go
So all looks are fair game
The same looks some get bullied for and called names
Are high fashion "urban chic" on the runway
Inspired by others looks, instant classic, embodying
    the human soul
They take it and shift it away
Then they change the name
While some can't get jobs with hair of a "different"
    name
So now corn rolls and boxer braids are cute
While black people's voices and culture is being
    muted
Yet it's undisputed who it came from
The name changed but the style's the same one

America is a sea of different colored faces
Same race
Hard working people trying to earn their place
No mistake
We are stronger by difference
Enriched
Heterogeneous
Specialization and diversification
Of a nation

Stripping America of its difference
Through viewing us through one lens
Even though what you see depends
On people's preferences, personal style, and general
    experience
They own their own human experience
Freedom is theirs
Freedoms of speech, religion, assembly, petition,
    press
That's the beauty of America:
We can speak out and not be oppressed
See our words are different, looks too, but we are one
So stop cultural appropriation and categorizing
    everyone
And expecting everyone to fit your one size
Then when they don't sit back and criticize
Them
For their own failure and inferiority
Judging a fish by its ability to climb a tree
Insisting you are sick of me
Of us
We are the problem
US
We are the problem

We need to fix the way we think and act and solve the
  problem
US

For Profit, Against Us

I'm a slave in my home
I hate that slave ship
Jump out and I drown
Stay in and I sink
Life for other's profit
I'm supposed to think
But not think
That's bad for profit
That's dangerous
But for who?
You and me both kid
So let's get this straight
The world is not straight
I can't think straight
With all these crooks and liars
Cheaters and beaters
The world is crooked
And I'm straight
To them I look bent
I must be fixed
Must be neutered and spayed
I can't stay
The way I am
There is money to be made

"It takes courage to grow up and turn out to be who

you really are"—**E.E. Cummings**

You?

Everyone everywhere
Has an opinion on who you should be
How to make you better
How to make you clearer
How you should come into focus
How to make you sharper
How to make you their own diamond
But it's up to you whether you listen
And why
Is it because you like it
Or them?
Is it to impress
Or to improve?
Do you know the reason
Or do you just do?
Are you sculpting yourself
Or are you being molded?
It takes courage to grow up
And stay being you
It takes courage to be an adult
And to decide to still be you

Dangerous Thoughts

How about we all be who we are regardless of stupid
    things like age and
Stand up for ourselves, and never stop growing and
    changing, but never be like anyone else either
If adulthood means giving up the magic in life and
    settling for the downward spiral and life in the
    cracks, then I failed at high school and I never
    learned my lesson
I've always dreaded being an adult because adulthood
    always seemed like death and monotony
But I've learned the secret and it was in me all along

Never Growing Old/Growing, but Never Old

I was born in the spring
A May flower in bloom
And my youth never dies
When I was born
I was born to rise
To change, to prosper, to get better
I was born to evolve and live forever
I see possibilities
From the ground to the trees
I see nature as both beauty and my playground

When I was a kid
I thought adults were born that way
Teachers lived at school
And had no outside life
And I would play at the park forever
As an older kid I feared adulthood
I thought other kids were unwise to want to leave
    their childhood behind
I thought: we don't pay taxes, we don't have kids, we
    don't work, and we don't have serious
    responsibilities
Why do other kids want to be big, when being big
    means you have to pay?
Apparently freedom to live and do things your way
    doesn't come cheap
And the typical adult would trade places with us any
    day
I thought it was sad that you had to give up playing
    hide and seek and going to the park because
    adults don't act that way

And I was sad that adulthood seemed to mean giving
     up your childhood
Then one day at the park with my daddy and brother,
I saw two adults get on the swings and leave
That gave me hope that I could swing forever and
     ever
Then I thought adulthood wouldn't be so bad
As long as they make swings then I could keep trying
     to touch the sky

When I was a tween I took a stand for my
     individuality
And gave some up in the process
To save the rest I had to butcher myself
I was perfect before
Now I am tainted by society
But still a gem, just not the one I was born
To survive life circumstances, sacrifices had to be
     made
But I stood up for who I am—short and brave
I loved to read and loved to learn
And my class was talented and brilliant
My middle school class was the best class of kids I've
     ever seen:
Ms. Blake and Mr. Miller, and 701 and 801 forever.
I didn't know it then but I would see Ramarley
     Graham once after we graduated and he'd be
     gone forever

I went to high school in Harlem and never came back

4 years of Adulthood Bootcamp changes people
    forever

Freshman year I made many friends and
    underachieved

But life was good and I wished it would stay that way
    forever

Sophomore year I got my act together, but everyone
    else fell by the wayside

Friends became hostile, adults stopped making sense,
    and I began to see the world unfolding

I took AP Government and Politics, Physics, English,
    and Algebra 2/Trigonometry, and argued a lot
    with Omar

There was lots of frustration, tears, failure, and
    character building, but I wasn't the only one who
    failed

In the end, I learned a lot but had nothing to show for
    it on paper except Robotics

But I developed as a person and helped build a robot

Junior year I learned to speak Harlem: I learned how
    to communicate with my peers and be taken
    seriously

I had long mastered speaking to adults and authority
    figures, but my peers always eluded me

I took up History Club and SAT prep, and had even
    more experiences

I was living my life, but Ramarley got shot by some
    cops up the block

Of course they got off

No justice no peace

But he wasn't special; urban kids have been slowly
    dying for a long time too

Just like my other friends; just like many before us

They just made it to senior year
I'm thinking about college and my SAT and future
    and some cops took away Ramarley's future for
    walking
I feared for my brother's safety walking the very
    streets we grew up walking
And realized just how unequal urban black kids were
Black President elected in 2008 and in 2011 there's
    stop and frisk, and hate
But life goes on, and more people slip farther into the
    cracks
But Ramarley lays submerged forever

Senior year I was grinding non stop
I took Psychology 201 at City College, the college
    engineering class at school, and AP Language
    and Composition
I kept up my extracurriculars and applied to 20
    colleges
That year was the year I was supposed to become an
    adult but 18 felt like 17 and nothing was special
    but how people started treating me
On my 18th birthday everyone said congratulations
    you're legal
Great so I can smoke tobacco and old dudes could
    date me without it being a crime
Thanks.
I had started reminiscing about life and what I had
    learned
Yeah legally I'm an adult, but am I ready to be?
Am I one in my mind?
I had been dreading the day
No way was I ever going to be old and jaded
But 18 came and I made some memories
And felt for my fallen homies dead or alive and gone

4 years of teaching you that everything before high
  school was a lie
And cramming "the real world" down your throat,
  and all I learned was I was right
Adulthood sucks and I never want to be one
Then I realized I needed to repeat middle school and
  stick with my childhood wisdom:
It is unwise to leave your childhood behind and even
  more unwise to change who you are because
  people tell you that you shouldn't be that way
If we all started acting our age then all young people
  would be carefree and irresponsible and all old
  people would be crotchety and curmudgeon
That's boring
And I refuse to be boring
So when I grow up I want to be an adult
But I will never embrace adulthood
I choose to define the person I want to be
And anyone who tells me I can't because it's wrong
  can shove off
I will do what I have been doing since I was born:
I am going to be me

Memorial Day/Graduation

To all my fallen soldiers
Now dead and gone
Fighting for life
You will always carry on
Born to die
Trying to live
Failing to survive
Yet still full of life
Your comrades remember you
Back in the day
Before talking to you
Meant speaking to your grave

Irresponsible

They say I'm irresponsible
These people I know
They're all the same:
Closed minded
They'll never know

I've been responsible since 3
Tiny person entrusted to me
Had to be a role model
Learned my piece
He always mirrored my bad
And ignored the good
And I learned just how hard responsibility could be
But I took it
Took care of it
I did my best
I learned

They say I'm irresponsible
But it's given
Not earned
Or so the irresponsible say
The drunk with authority
Those who don't wear it well
These responsibilities
They bear it
They complain it
They wear it
They tear it
They rip it
They throw it in your face
Like shreds are leverage
They are but average

Throwing "responsibility" in your face

Those who mirror you
Respect you
Who give you authority
They see
They watch
They mimic
They question
Make excuses?
Throw tantrums?
Don't listen?
Are you a man?
Are you a woman?
Are you an adult?
Are you in charge
At all?

It was a question
An insight
Why does your authority bite?
Why does subordination threaten you?
Why are you a savage?
What did I do?
I questioned your "authority"
That was given
Not earned
And instead of just answering
You felt your cheeks burn
How dare I be right?
Or question the norm?
Or make you think?
Or talk at all?

Curiosity stinks to the responsible dictator
When they dictate and you ask
And you have done no wrong
But you're wrong
Always wrong
You offended their values
They do
Not think
They expect the same from you
They told you what to do
They told you how it is
They told you what to be
And you dared to ask why
Are you crazy?

People have died for doing what you've done
But this is America
You have that right
Because you are right
You questioned
You asked
So in wrong you are right
They may have their reasons
But a question isn't a threat
Except to the weak who are easily threatened
Goes to show the power of unearned authority
Or respect

You undermine them with your power
Because you do have power
One they'll never understand
You are a leader
Not by circumstance
Not because of your age
Or because you had sex
But because you have character
And that is not given
They say I'm irresponsible
But I'll never give in

Know Yourself

To know God is to know yourself and to know
    yourself is to know God
To know your purpose, to know your destiny, to
    know who you are
To be self-aware, to shine bright as a star
Think about it:
To be the best you have to know who you are

Black Girl Classic

My future is my present and my past I'm timeless
My future is my present and my past I'm timeless
They say I'm lost
They say I've forgotten
But I've been doing me since the dawn of time
I was Eve in the Eden the original mother
I am royalty
I was the longest running Egyptian queen
So bad they called me King
I was beautiful and powerful as Queen Nefertiti
And as Cleopatra
I was stolen and drowning in the Atlantic Ocean
But I survived and emerged as powerful as ever
They tried to break me and rape me until my culture
        was raped away
They told me I had no history and I was out of place
They had me confused and speaking new tongues
That seemed to leave me lost in translation
They pressed me til I Pressed my tresses
They left me stressed and feeling oppressed
So I sang the blues in this strange new tongue
I made lemons into lemonade and sang of "Strange
        Fruit"
I was Billie Holiday and Marian Anderson
New look, new culture, new language, new me
But I missed the old look of an African queen
So I dug deep and found soul
I was Nina Simone
I had soul glow and my Fro
I am Black Power
But everything wasn't Straight
So I became Rosa Parks and Coretta Scott King
And there I was again

40

They loved me and they Dreaded me
Their knickers were in a bunch when my hair was in a
    Knot
So I Wrapped it, transformed it and became Beyoncé
And gained mass appeal
Then I got political and became Michelle Obama
I had people sayin I was Wavy, and I knew I was
    Straight
I rediscovered myself and remembered I am cultured
Now I'm Straight, Wavy, and I got them Twisted
Then I look around at myself making a presence
And I remember
My future is my present and my past I'm timeless

You, Me, We

I look at you and see the world
I see my soul, I see me
How could I look at you and not love you like me?
Created an image one of God
One
We are Gods
Hearts without borders
No applause
Let's start living right off stage
Kindness lost
Slipped so far we have to generate it randomly
Just to keep hope alive in humanity
Stop asking "what would Jesus do?"
And start asking what will you do?
We are Gods
Create your own image
You have agency
You can write the play and not be the puppet
You can make the stage
You can hold the strings
You can compose the music
You can see all the things
Others can't
Make them see
You are here
Be all you can be
I look at you and see the world
I see my soul, I see me

Human Museum

I see faces
Beautiful works of art
Lines soft and sharp
Beautiful in both symmetry and asymmetry
Of different shades and hues
I see you
What you present and represent
Your expression
Your soul worn on your sleeve and body
Covered up to blend into the moving still life
Evolving yet unchanging
Ugly but still beautiful
I see hidden gems
I see love and friendship
I see lines blurring
I see new and old combining to make beautiful new
    works of art
I see green, I see blue, I see brown, I see your souls
Staring at me and they're beautiful
Different orbs of mystery and untold secrets
I see whole pictures and tiny details
I see slashed lines and cover ups
Little and big injustices and indecencies
Insults to art, to who we are
And when I look in the mirror
I see me on the periphery
Connected but somehow not
I am not the only one here
But it seems like it
The illusion is great
It's beautiful and sad
What it must be like to be a central part of the
    tapestry!

43

But I am but loosely connected by a thread
Wondering how being interwoven must feel
I see your faces, lives, and souls blurring together
Yet I am just an onlooker staring in awe at your
      museum
Your delicate works of art

Daydream

I make myself laugh
I make myself cry
I make myself brave
I make myself hide
Imagination vivid
I walk on the edge
Of fantasy reality
Of real and pretend
I pretend people are real
I pretend they care
I pretend they are worth it
I pretend self-interest fails
In this society does alTru-ism
Really prevail?
I guess I hope so
If not then we all fail
We need each other to make it
No matter what they say
Although now we stand on each other
And we are all in the way
We can learn to work together
In work and in play
I believe in the people
I believe in myself
I believe in a world worth living in together
I believe in peace
I believe in happiness
I believe we can survive the belly of the beast

UNITY

UNITY
U N I TOGETHER Y?
Because U N I Together forms UNIT
Because U N I mean cohesiveness and teamwork
IT means community
IT means pull yourselves up by your bootstraps,
    Together
IT means we go farther than you and me
IT means "I, Too, Sing America" and "I Have a
    Dream"
IT means we work Together, we play Together, we
    succeed Together, we are Together
Y UNITEveryone?
Because we are already one
And once we are UNITED we will have already won

No Love

So you look around wondering "where is the love?
Where is your love? Is there any love around?"
But you never had to look for it should be within
Beautiful eyes, Beautiful soul
Most look outward with negative eyes
Yet expect others to see past their flaws
If you live in love you shall find love everywhere
If you live in negativity then that shall follow too

A Lesson in Relationships

Any relationship is defined by U N I
But without context U and I are just two letters
Just an incomplete word
Context is a variable N that must be understood
Our relationship situation between U and I can be
Big (N)
Or Small (n)
But whether you think in letters and words
Or in numbers, graphs, and curves
One thing is certain
N is always a variable between U aNd I
Knowing this we can UNIte
We can foster commUNIty
I can befrIeNd U
And not be daUNted by the dIstance
BecaUse we kNow Its place
It can never be erased
All we can do is work with it
It fUNctIons INdependently of Us

Siddhartha

I'm a wanderer
Gautama when I walk through
I'm a princess in excess
I excel in seeing suffering
I'm tired of the suffering
The crying of my people
It's Nirvana when I speak truths
We need action
And I'm not done traveling

Internal vs. External Locus

God was lost
People claimed to know where God was and who God
    is
But their actions were subhuman
People were seeking God
Searching among humans
They were confused
They heard we were created in God's image
They looked around trying to root out the imposters
But God was not free
God was held captive
A prison of the body
Won't you let God free every once in a while?
Searching for God's vision, they didn't see it in the
    mirror
They did not dig deep to make it clearer
They didn't search their soul so they search for
    something they always had
They never looked inward to find God imprisoned
    inside them
If they did then God would show in their actions like
    the elect
But they don't know God
They haven't gotten in touch with themselves
So even to the "saved"
God remains in jail

The Path

I was walking down this path
I cannot see the end of
I know the end of this path will come
But until then I still walk

I do not feel the need to walk continuously
Sometimes I sit
Sometimes I stop and look around
Sometimes I sleep

Some believe they have to take a specific path
Some believe they can make their own
Some think they can take many paths
Some believe they can switch

Then they get to the end
Many realize all they did was walk
Many wonder what if they'd taken another
"Should I have ran or napped instead?!"

They are dead
Waiting for their perception of God to arrive
Some did not live or even watch others live
They never even questioned why they were walking

What if they veered into the wilderness?
How do they know they walked right?
They thought walking would definitively keep them
        ahead
But it was the ones who ventured who created the
        path they walked

Holy War

Your war is holy
But what kills me is
Murder is a sin
Forgive me

Some Politics

Killing yourself was illegal
Why?
Because we are property of the government
That's why we still send our young people to die in
    squabbles of the elite
And spend taxpayer dollars on our own defeat
But not on our uplift
No education fi di yutes
Number 17 on the list but we spend the most money
A whole two thousand more on white than black
    children
But more than the next 8 countries combined on our
    military
Like pawns on a chess board for our leaders to send a
    message:
"I told you so!"
What for?
We really could be the best
But instead of thinking west
Maybe we should think north

No Regrets

I'm moving on
I'm letting go
I've washed away
What I've done
The sins of my sons
The sins of my fathers
Infractions past
Regrets lost
Getting sleep
Living life
It's my soul to keep

Siddhartha of the Hood

I'm wandering
I'm wondering
Who is the hood?
When is the peace?
Where are we going?
Why am I going?
Is it the same place?
I see everything and nothing
All in the same place

Hoodlum (noun):

A person who engages in crime and violence; a

hooligan or gangster.

You Hoodlum?

I didn't really know what a hoodlum was til I looked
    it up
I didn't think it was a criminal or a violent person
I guess I thought it was a kid from the hood
What society paints hoodlums as
But I knew I wasn't and I knew the difference
If someone calls me a hoodlum
I inform them they are wrong
Clearly they don't know what a real hoodlum is
I'm no miscreant
Yet somehow hoodlum is cool
Like a reclaimed word
Like nigger
Word
It's something we call ourselves
But don't you do that
You don't know what one is
You don't get it
I guess to know a hoodlum one must be from the
    hood

Mis-Hoodlum

White people call me a hoodlum
Because in the suburbs I stand out
White people call me sassy
'Cause all this black can't be held
I wonder if they know what a real hoodlum looks like
Or is it the hoodie that I actually wear on my head
Because only hoodlums do that
Do they know that being from the hood doesn't make
    you a hoodlum?
Do they know in the hood I was an Oreo?
I'm too white for black people yet too black for white
    people
Guess it good I'm from the Bronx
There's always Hispanics

Polo Ground Rules

There's rules to the hood
How you walk
How you talk
We know when you're from here
So don't mess up
If you're not from here
You're cool if you're not scared of hoodlums
If you're not like "these niggers
These spics, those hoodboogers"
But look scared and it's fatal
Your ignorance kills
Or at least leaves you broke
And lost in the hood
Don't treat us like savages
And we'll let you pass
But act wrong in the hood
And we'll show you some act right
Don't walk too fast
Don't walk too slow
Don't avoid looking at someone
But don't look at them either
It's an art and a skill
We know it's extra
But that's how it is
If you don't wanna get hurt

Scars and Invisible Ink

Fucked up
Yeah there's proof
But not enough
Scars left
And tattoos
You can't see it
Yet you can
All demeanor
Visible imprint
Left in pieces
Secretly tatted
Life's wearing on me
Life's writing on me
The writing's on my heart
The writing's in my brain
The writing's on my sleeve
It's in my skin
Life's cloaking me
Society is skin deep
But I go deeper
My tattoos may be permanent
But you can't see them

Thinking

I've been thinking
It's painful sometimes
Very seldom it moves me to tears

I've been thinking bout Rachel
And I cried my eyes out
How I love and miss you so
I've been thinking bout Omar, Ramarley, and Taj
And all the ghetto youths trying to survive
How can I make it easier for you?

I've been thinking bout the world
Little kids dying from lack of clean water and
    electricity
Yet do we care in this first world democracy?

I've been thinking bout the lies that we tell our
    citizens
And how hard it is to make people believe the truth
It's gonna be a hard life arguing with you

I've been thinking bout everything
The world is on my shoulders
But then again it's on yours too so you should be
    thinking too

Little Me, P.S. 103

I remember when my school mascot was a bumblebee
Little kids, Little me
They told us to be visionaries and to think BIG
Dream Big, Work Hard
I remember when my school mascot was a sunflower
New Principal, New Mascot
They told us to grow tall and reach for the sky
Like Woody from *Toy Story*
I remember going to P.S. 103 and being bullied
Big thinker, Too small
I remember Ramarley Graham being popular
Here today, Gone tomorrow
I remember being IMMORTAL and always alive
Sticks and Stones, No broken bones
I remember being STRONG and vowing to stay me
Still dreaming, Still working
I remember being done but not done—never finished
Still learning, Still growing

Carpenter Avenue

Yeah we're hard
And we'll chop you down
Form you to what we want
Makin it good
Everything you need on this street in the hood
Or up the block
That's White Plains
Got the whole world on the block or on the train
Schools and hospitals
Montefiore
Raised up through here
Yeah I had it made
A tree in the Bronx grew on Carpenter
Got cut down
Became something else
We'll see what I made

Masquerading Marauder

I'm a masquerading marauder
I change my face in different places
I seek new adventures
New faces
New places
It's my major advantage
I'm reading you like a book
But you can't read me
I transform then I'm gone

See I speak benevolent
Like I have a daydream
No I have a vision
Like none you have seen

I speak malevolent like
Blow that shit up
Burn that shit down
But switch to create something new

I masquerade as straight ugly
And I see how that goes
Then I switch it to queer beauty
And I see how that goes

I speak gibberish and niggerish
Like "who's the bitch?"
Like "facts niggas ain't shit"
Like "Aow aha word"

I speak eloquently like
If you have no vision you are blind
I tell 'em if you can see yourself you see the world—
you see stars
But with no vision you are blind
We are lost

I speak queer like
They/Them Ze/Hir is so aware of who they are
Their inner beauty is so inspiring
Pronouns don't mean shit when You and I is right

I speak New York like
What's good B?
Word? Facts! It's lit
But wait deadass?
Yo run that shit
Word? Facts

I speak America like
Tennis shoes and Orange coke
And whole pies—no pizza by the slice
And no deli's

I change my look like
Pimpin' pimpin'
Killin these hoes
Then to a bad bitch
Showing off no insecurities

I transform too
From a tomboy
To a "lady"
Lady like looks
Are a costume
Women wear well

I see through all these looks
And these different speeches
'Cause I'm watching
I'm reading your books
And I'm turning your pages
I'm looking at your cover
But I'm trying to uncover you
Discover you

I'm reading your words, your sentences, your lines,
    your lies, your illustrations

Those illusions

I'm drawing conclusions

And I'm adding to my faces

So when I go to different places I know what I see

Know who to be

I'm learning and I'm writing, but I'm not done
    reading

I'm masquerading as whatever to uncover your
    secrets

99 Problems and Being a Bitch is One

Having a vagina is like being born with a bullet
    wound that never heals
Never not been shot so I don't know how it feels
To be treated like a whole person yeah I know the
    deal
No one wants the disabled yeah I know how it feels
They don't wanna hire us and so we don't get paid
Missing my 22 cents I keeps getting played
Growing up they told me that girls don't play
So we're sitting on the bench while the boys all play
Loser mentality
To compete you have to play
Cultivating weakness while ignoring our strengths
Just hand us a tampon and say: "sit on the bench
Be seen and not heard
Beauty is in the eyes of the beholder
Make as many behold you as possible"
It's absurd
"No man has never noticed a lady's inner beauty"
    they say
And so we stay insecure trying to patch up our
    wounds
No oozing
Trying to make you see we're not losing
No fooling
Less clothes just to show we're bold—nothing to hide
Acting
No secrets, no lies
In fact—
We didn't see who we could be 'cause we were
caught up in who we are
We were taught to be less than
And the finish line is far

67

A Woman's Place

If God made man in his image then what are we?
Women.
Does that mean that is all we were meant to be?
Are women supposed to be a second class to men?
Are we supposed to act our part and say:
"Keep the 22 cents?"
Not tenacious or aggressive
So we live on the fence
While the men reap the garden of the plants we sowed
After we played our part
They hunted what we gathered
And eat what we planted
I cannot understand it

"Equality is a commodity."—**Walter Mosley**

The Feminine Equation

These girls are basic like 2+2
Yet they can't even which is odd
When their potential is limitless
Like increasing without bound
When the limit does not exist
Gender conditioning persists
Keeping our ladies in place
But equality in our face

I Own My Labor (In My Dreams)

I don't ever wanna work for someone else

Out here slaving while they increasin in wealth

Keep me busy, undermine me, take my rights on the
  stealth

Mode on survival: I hung my dreams on the shelf

And put 'em in a casket

Ashes to ashes dust to dreams

I hide there trick

Or treat

So when we leave

Surprise!

That's right:

My dreams and I, we are still alive

They thought they broke me but still I rise

I might be broke but never broken

They can't tell me who to be

Broke Girl Blues

I told myself to write more and think less
I'm stressed out trying to work hard to be the best
Trying to work hard in school but it's a test
Trying to work way more and sleep less
But homework and money make me sleepless
Meanwhile I'm anemic so all I do is sleep
And broke college student food makes me weak
Iron pills in the trash don't help me get ahead
All these things mean is anywhere is my bed
I sleep like I'm narcoleptic while trying to get ahead
I'm just trying every day to be more than fed
No dreams deferred here
I'll graduate from Harlem twice
So here goes nothing
I have get this right

Peasant

I am what you call a "peasant"
Look at me
I am
Tattered clothing
Unkempt
This can't have a justification
This can't have a rationale
I don't exist
Not in America
Because I am a voice
A mind
I exemplify opportunity
Wasted
Look at me
I'm holey
I live despite my sins
I fail to follow the rules
But I move forward
I exist
On the street
But not in our mind
The collective
The peasant failed
Or chose this life
Their was education

And wealth

And training

You know home

That taught

How to dress

Who to be

How to act

And they failed

I failed

Look at me

I'm wrong

Who dresses like this?

Who is proud of that?

How did I become this?

Where's my agency?

I let my bootstraps get worn

I let them get torn off

It is my fault I have no bootstraps to pull myself up
    by

If my clothes get holey-er

It's my fault

I didn't preserve what I had

Or didn't

And when I can't get hired

Because I don't look middle class

It's my fault

For thinking

73

Looking
Dressing like a peasant
And when I die
Like a peasant
With no money for my funeral
From the cold hard world
That my holey clothes couldn't protect me from
It will be my fault for not adapting
I will not exist
No scourge for you to look at
Those failures who didn't get it
Their piece of American wealth
The knowledge is their(s)
And I chose not to own it
So I kept myself down
Why couldn't I live an unholey existence?
I am what we don't see
What we don't talk about
The grace amongst the disgraced

The Mask

I saw you masking your pain
A task you did in vain

A Thank You Note

Special thanks to Lawrence Joy for doing my cover for me, my friends and family for the support, and my parents, both for raising me to believe I can do anything I set my mind to and for raising me to believe that I am not inferior to anyone and that we are all created equal. I would also like to thank all my teachers, including life, for getting me this far. And last but certainly not least, thank you Lisa (Crosswell) for editing my book for me. You're a lifesaver.

About the Author

Stacy St. Hilaire is a senior sociology major at the City College of New York with an interest in structural inequality. Her essay *Marcus Garvey: From Jamaican Peasant to Potent World Leader* is featured on Dale Shield's iForColor.org, and she has contributed numerous articles and videos on the 18 Karat Reggae platform using the pseudonym Bronx Girl.

Made in the USA
Middletown, DE
17 September 2018